FRANKENSTEIN

There are probably more films of this sad and frightening story than of any other story in the world. Why do so many people like it? Is it because Frankenstein's monster is something we all know, something from our worst dreams?

It is an old story, and a new story – 'old' because it was written more than 180 years ago; 'new' because Frankenstein's problem is the same problem that scientists have today. Science gives us many wonderful discoveries – machines, computers, weapons – but how do we use these things? Will they give us a better life, or will they destroy us in the end?

Victor Frankenstein creates a new man, bigger and stronger than any other man – a huge and frightening monster. But even monsters need love, and when his creator turns away from him, the monster begins to destroy everything that Frankenstein loves . . .

T0355166

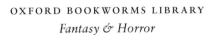

OXFORD BOOKWORMS LIBRARY

Fantasy & Horror

Frankenstein

Stage 3 (1000 headwords)

Series Editor: Jennifer Bassett
Founder Editor: Tricia Hedge
Activities Editors: Jennifer Bassett and Alison Baxter

MARY SHELLEY

Frankenstein

Retold by
Patrick Nobes

OXFORD UNIVERSITY PRESS

OXFORD
UNIVERSITY PRESS

Great Clarendon Street, Oxford, OX2 6DP, United Kingdom

Oxford University Press is a department of the University of Oxford.
It furthers the University's objective of excellence in research, scholarship,
and education by publishing worldwide. Oxford is a registered trade
mark of Oxford University Press in the UK and in certain other countries

This simplified edition © Oxford University Press 2008

The moral rights of the author have been asserted

First published in Oxford Bookworms 1989

52

ISBN: 978 0 19 479116 8   Book
ISBN: 978 0 19 462097 0   Book and audio pack

Printed in China

Word count (main text): 9,685 words

For more information on the Oxford Bookworms Library,
visit www.oup.com/elt/gradedreaders

ACKNOWLEDGEMENTS

Text adapted by Patrick Nobes

Illustrated by Lynd Ward, courtesy of the Bodleian Library, Oxford
(Shelf mark 256 d 585; pp. 5, 10, 11, 26, 44, 53, 70, 90, 106, 110, 114,
124, 150, 160, 162, 170, 186, 188, 200, 216, 223, 226, 232, 242)

The publishers have made every effort to contact the copyright holder
of the illustrations, but have been unable to do so. If the copyright
holder would like to contact the publishers, the publishers
would be happy to pay an appropriate reproduction fee.

Cover image from JJs courtesy of Alamy

CONTENTS

'Captain! Something is moving on the ice. Look over there!'

The sailor stood at the top of the mast, high above the Captain. His hand pointed away from the ship, across the miles of ice that covered the sea.

The Captain looked to the north, where the sailor was pointing. He saw something coming fast towards the ship across the ice. He put his telescope to his eye, and through it he could see the shapes of ten dogs pulling a sledge over the ice. He could also see the driver of the sledge – a huge figure, much bigger than a man.

The sledge came nearer and nearer to the sea. Soon it was only a quarter of a mile from the ship. No one

'Captain! Something is moving on the ice. Look over there!'

needed a telescope now to see the huge figure of the driver.

Suddenly the sledge went behind a mountain of ice and disappeared. At that moment another sledge appeared. It, too, was moving fast, and was clearly chasing the first sledge. This driver was a smaller figure, more like an ordinary man. Faster and faster the dogs ran; then the second sledge also disappeared behind the mountain of ice.

Two hours passed. The sledges did not appear again. Nothing moved on the ice. Soon night came, and in the night there was a storm. In the morning, the sailors saw that great pieces of ice were floating round the ship. Suddenly the sailor on the mast shouted again.

'Captain, I can see a man on the ice.'

The sailor was pointing to a piece of ice that was floating near the ship. A man was sitting on the ice, and near him

Soon night came, and in the night there was a storm.

was a broken sledge. The man was nearly dead from cold and could not walk. The sailors carried him carefully on to the ship, and took him to the Captain, who said:

'Welcome to my ship. I am the Captain and my name is Robert Walton.'

'Thank you, Captain Walton,' the man said. 'My name is Frankenstein, Victor Frankenstein.'

Then he fainted and said no more.

Two days passed before the man was strong enough to talk and then the Captain asked him to tell his story.

'I am trying to catch someone,' said Frankenstein. 'That is why I have come so far north on the ice.'

'We saw you following someone,' the Captain said. 'He was huge, much bigger than a man. We saw his sledge just in front of you on the night before the storm.'

'I am pleased you all saw that huge figure,' Frankenstein said. 'Perhaps that will help you to believe my story.'

During the days, while the Captain worked on the ship, Frankenstein wrote down his story, and each evening he read what he had written to the Captain.

Here is Victor Frankenstein's story.

Victor Frankenstein's Story Begins

2

I was born in Switzerland, in the town of Geneva. My parents loved each other very much, and I learnt from the example of their love. I learnt that to love and to be patient are the most important things in the world.

My mother hoped to have a daughter after I was born, but for five years I was the only child. And then my mother found a sister for me. She was helping a family in which there were five children. They were very poor, and the children were thin and hungry. One of the children was a little girl, with golden hair and blue eyes. Her name was Elizabeth. My mother took the little girl into our family, and Elizabeth became the daughter that my mother had always wanted. As I grew older, my love for Elizabeth became stronger all the time.

Later my mother had two other sons, Ernest and William. A young woman called Justine came to live in the house to help my mother with the children. We loved her as much as she loved us.

The years passed happily, and we had everything that we needed. At school I met another very fine person. His name was Henry Clerval, and he was very clever. My family also liked him very much, so he was a welcome visitor to our house.

One of the children was a little girl, with golden hair and blue eyes.
Her name was Elizabeth.

I studied very hard at school. I wanted to know the secrets of life, and, most of all, I wanted to know how to make living things. I read all the books that I could find. One day, something happened that added a new idea to the ideas that I already had. I was fifteen at the time, and we were on holiday in the mountains. There was a wild storm, and with it came the most frightening thunder and lightning that I have ever seen in my life. About twenty metres in front of our house was a great tree. Suddenly a huge fork of lightning hit the tree. After a few seconds, there was nothing left of it except a black piece of wood two metres high. The lightning had destroyed it.

I saw how strong electricity was. I began to read all the books that I could find about electricity and its terrible power.

3

For seventeen years my life was very happy. Then the first sad thing happened. My mother became very ill, and soon she knew that she was dying. Just before she died, she asked Elizabeth and me to go to her room. She held our hands and said:

'My children, I am very happy because you love each other, and because one day you will get married. Everyone in the family loves you, Elizabeth. Will you take my place in the family, my dear? I can die happy if you will look after them when I have gone.'

My mother died, and we were very sad, because we loved her dearly. Elizabeth was brave and helped us; her sweet smile gave us some happiness in the unhappy days after my mother's death.

The time came for me to go to university. I did not want to leave my sad family, but we all knew that I should go. It was hard to leave, too, because the parents of my good friend Henry Clerval would not let him go to university with me. And so I had to go alone.

On my first day at the university I met my teacher, Professor Waldman, who was one of the greatest scientists in the world. He gave a wonderful talk to all the students who were starting at the university. He ended his talk by saying: 'Some of you will become the great scientists of tomorrow. You must study hard and discover everything that you can. That is why God made you intelligent – to help other people.'

After the professor's talk, I thought very carefully. I remembered the storm when I was fifteen. I remembered how the lightning had destroyed the tree. I wanted to use electricity to help people, and I wanted to discover the secrets of life. I decided to work on these two things. I did not know then that my work would destroy me and the people that I loved.

I started work the next day. I worked very hard and soon Professor Waldman and I realized that I could learn to be a very good scientist.

The professor helped me very much, and other important

How does life begin? Is it possible to put life into dead things?

scientists who were his friends helped me, too. I was interested in my work and I did not take one day's holiday during the next two years. I did not go home, and my letters to my family were very short.

After two years I had discovered many things and I built a scientific machine that was better than anything in the university. My machine would help me answer the most important question of all. How does life begin? Is it possible to put life into dead things? To answer these questions about life I had to learn first about death. I had to watch bodies from the moment when they died and the warm life left them. In the hospital and in the university, I watched the dying and the dead. Day after day, month after month, I followed death. It was a dark and terrible time.

Then one day, the answer came to me. Suddenly I was sure that I knew the secret of life. I knew that I could put life into a body that was not alive.

I worked harder and harder now. I slept for only a short time each night, and I did not eat much food. I wrote to my family less often. But they loved me and did not stop writing to me. They said they understood how busy I was. They did not want me to stop work to write or to see them. They would wait until I had more time. They hoped to see me very soon.

The professors realized that I was doing very important work, and so they gave me my own laboratory. There was a small flat above the laboratory, where I lived, and sometimes I stayed inside the building for a week and did not go out.

Above the laboratory I built a very tall mast. It was 150 metres high, and higher than the tallest building in the city. The mast could catch lightning and could send the electricity down to my machine in the laboratory. I had never forgotten the lightning that had destroyed the tree. There had been so much power in the electricity of that lightning. I believed I could use that electricity to give life to things that were dead.

I will say no more than that. The secret of my machine must die with me. I was a very clever scientist, but I did not realize then what a terrible mistake I was making.

4

In my laboratory I made a body. I bought or stole all the pieces of human body that I needed, and slowly and carefully, I put them all together.

I did not let anybody enter my laboratory or my flat while I was doing this awful work. I was afraid to tell anybody my terrible secret.

I had wanted to make a beautiful man, but the face of the creature was horrible. Its skin was thin and yellow, and its eyes were as yellow as its skin. Its long black hair and white teeth were almost beautiful, but the rest of the face was very ugly.

Its legs and arms were the right shape, but they were huge. I had to use big pieces because it was too difficult to

I bought or stole all the pieces of human body that I needed.

join small pieces together. My creature was two and a half metres tall.

For a year I had worked to make this creature, but now it looked terrible and frightening. I almost decided to destroy it. But I could not. I had to know if I could put life into it.

I joined the body to the wires from my machine. More wires joined the machine to the mast. I was sure that my machine could use electricity from lightning to give life to the body. I watched and waited. Two days later I saw dark clouds in the sky, and I knew that a storm was coming. At about one o'clock in the morning the lightning came. My mast began to do its work immediately, and the electricity from the lightning travelled down the mast to my machine. Would the machine work?

At first nothing happened. But after a few minutes I saw the creature's body begin to move. Slowly, terribly, the body came alive. Its arms and legs began to move, and slowly it sat up.

The dead body had been an ugly thing, but alive, it was much more horrible. Suddenly I wanted to escape from it. I ran out of the laboratory, and locked the door. I was filled with fear at what I had done.

For hours I walked up and down in my flat. At last I lay down on my bed, and fell asleep. But my sleep was full of terrible dreams, and I woke up suddenly. The horrible thing that I had created was standing by my bed. Its yellow eyes were looking at me; its mouth opened and it made strange sounds at me. On its yellow face there was an awful smile. One of its huge hands reached towards me . . .

Before it could touch me, I jumped off the bed and ran downstairs into the garden. I stayed there all night, but I could not think clearly. I was afraid. And when morning came, I went out into the town and began to walk about.

I did not notice where I was walking, but soon I came to the station. A train from Geneva had just arrived, and the passengers were leaving the station. One of them ran towards me when he saw me. It was my dear friend Henry Clerval.

He was very pleased to see me. He took my hand and shook it warmly.

'My dear Victor!' he said. 'What a lucky chance that you are here at the station. Your father, and Elizabeth and the others, are very worried about you, because you have not visited them for a long time. They asked me to make sure that you are well. And I have very good news. My father has agreed to let me study at the university, so we shall be able to spend a lot of time together.'

I was very happy to hear this news, and for a moment I forgot my fears. I took Henry back to my flat and asked him to wait outside while I went in to look. I was afraid that the creature was still there. But it had disappeared. At that time I did not think of other people, and what the creature could do to them. I took Henry into the flat and cooked a meal for us. But Henry noticed how thin I was, and that I was laughing too much and could not sit still.

Suddenly he said: 'My dear Victor, what is the matter with you? Are you ill? Has something awful happened?'

'Don't ask me that,' I cried. I put my hands over my eyes. I thought I could see the horrible creature there in front of me. I pointed wildly across the room, and shouted: 'He can tell you. Save me! Save me!' I tried to fight the creature, but there was nothing there. Then I fainted and fell to the floor.

Poor Henry! I do not know what he thought. He called a doctor and they put me to bed. I was very ill for two months, and Henry stayed and looked after me. His loving care saved me from death.

I wanted to go home and see my family as soon as possible. When I was well enough, I packed my clothes and books. All my luggage was ready, and I was feeling very happy when the postman arrived with some letters. One of the letters ended my short time of happiness.

5

The letter was from my father in Geneva, and this is what he wrote:

My dear Victor,
I want you to know before you arrive home that an awful thing has happened. Your dear youngest

13

brother, William, is dead. He was murdered. It
happened last Thursday evening when Elizabeth and
I and your two brothers, Ernest and William, went
for a walk outside the city. William and Ernest were
playing. William had hidden from Ernest, and
Ernest asked Elizabeth and me to help find William.
We all began to search for him, but we couldn't find
him. We searched all night. At five in the morning I
found him. He was lying on the grass, white and
still. I could see the marks of fingers on his neck –
the murderer had strangled him.

Elizabeth had let him wear a gold chain of hers
round his neck. On the chain was a very small
picture of your mother. We all think that someone
murdered William to steal the gold chain. Poor
Elizabeth is terribly unhappy at William's death. She
thinks he died because she let him wear the chain.
Hurry home, my dear Victor. You are the only one
who can help Elizabeth, and we all need you.

With all our love,
Your Father

Henry helped me to catch the train. The journey seemed
very long, and it was late at night before the train reached
Geneva. I decided to spend the night in a village outside the
town and go home early in the morning. I wanted to see the
place where William had died.

As I started my walk, a storm broke and lightning lit the

'Poor Elizabeth is terribly unhappy at William's death.'

sky. The police had put posts round the place where the murderer had strangled William, so I found it easily. I cried sadly as I stood there. My poor brother had been a kind and happy boy, and we had all loved him.

Again the lightning lit the sky, and I saw a huge figure standing in the rain. When I saw it, I knew at once what it was. It was the creature that I had made.

What was he doing there? But although I asked myself the question, I knew the answer. He had murdered my brother. I was sure that I was right.

I decided to try and catch him. But as I moved, he ran towards the mountains. He ran much faster than any man. He climbed the mountain easily, reached the top, and disappeared.

I stood there in the dark and the rain, and knew that I had created a monster. And he had murdered my brother.

*I saw a huge figure standing in the rain. It was the creature
that I had made.*

6

A t first I decided to tell the police my story. But would they believe me? I had been very ill. When the police learnt about my illness, they would think the monster was just one of my bad dreams. I decided that I could not tell anybody.

I went home to my family and they were very pleased to see me. Then they told me that the police had found the murderer. Perhaps you will think that this was good news, but I have not told you who the police had arrested.

As I went into the house, I noticed that one person did not come to meet me. It was Justine, the young woman who looked after the children and who was like a sister to us. And it was Justine that the police had arrested.

A few days after the murder, the police had searched the house and had found the gold chain in Justine's coat pocket. Everyone in the family knew that Justine had not murdered William. I knew who the murderer was, but I could not tell anyone. We were sure that Justine would be free after the trial, because nobody could believe that she was a murderer. But we were wrong.

The trial did not go well for Justine. There were a number of strange facts that were difficult to explain, and the judge decided that she was the murderer. The punishment for murder was death. We argued and cried.

We said she could not murder anyone. But nothing could change the judge's order. So I got up early and went to the judge's house and told him about the monster. He did not believe me. He thought I was lying in order to save Justine's life.

In the prison Justine waited quietly for death. We spent many hours with her, and she spoke calmly and kindly to us. She was happy because we believed that she had not killed William. And she was almost looking forward to death, because then she would be with William and our dear mother in a place of peace.

Her love and gentleness added to my great unhappiness. I knew she was going to die because of me. I knew my brother had died because of me. I had brought nothing but sadness and misery to my family.

I took a boat and went out on Lake Geneva. Why didn't I end my life then? Two things stopped me. My father was old and another death would probably kill him. And I had to stay alive – to keep my family safe from the monster.

Fear for my family and hate for my monster were with me day and night. I became ill again, and Elizabeth's love could not help me. I needed to escape for a while – to leave my unhappiness behind me. So I went to walk alone in the Alps. I hoped the wild beauty of the mountains would help me.

Slowly I became calmer among the beautiful mountains. I learnt to sleep again, and for days I did not see anybody.

In the prison Justine waited quietly for death.

Then one morning I saw a figure coming towards me faster than any man could go. It jumped easily over the rocks and I saw with horror the monster that I had created. On his face was a look of deep sadness, but also of evil. At first I could not speak because I hated him so much. But at last I said:

'You are an evil creature. I shall kill you if I can, because you have killed two people that I love.'

The monster's yellow eyes looked at me. 'I am the unhappiest creature in the world, but I shall fight for my life,' he said. 'I am bigger and stronger than you, but I will not start the fight. I shall always be gentle to you because you are my king and creator. You made me, and you should love me and be kind to me, like a father. William and Justine died because you did not love me. Why did you create me if you were not ready to love me?'

'We are enemies,' I said. 'Leave me now, or let us fight

'I am the unhappiest creature in the world,' the monster said.

20

until one of us is dead. You are a murderer. How can I be kind to you?'

'You say *I* am a murderer,' the monster said, 'but *you* want to kill your own creature. Isn't that wrong, too? I ask you to do one thing for me – listen. Come with me to a warmer place, and listen to my story. Then you can decide.'

I thought carefully about what he had said. It was true that I had given him life but I had not given him love. I decided to go with him and listen to his story.

He took me to a mountain hut where he lit a fire. We sat down by the fire and he began to tell me his story.

The Monster's Story

7

After I had left the laboratory, I escaped into the country outside the town. I soon felt hungry and thirsty, and my first food was fruit which I found on some trees near a river. I drank from the river and then lay down and went to sleep.

At first my eyes and ears did not work very well, but after a while I began to see and hear clearly.

One day, snow began to fall. Of course, I had never walked in snow before, and I found that it made my feet very cold. I realized that I needed food and a place to get warm. Soon I saw a small hut where an old man was cooking his breakfast over a fire. When the old man saw me, he shouted loudly and ran away as fast as he could. I did not understand what the man was doing, but I wanted to be near the fire. So I sat down in the warm, and ate the man's breakfast. Then I walked across empty fields for some hours until I reached a village. I went into one of the houses, but there were children inside. They began to scream when they saw me, and their mother fainted. The whole village came to see what was the trouble. Some of the people ran away when they saw me, but the others shouted and threw stones at me. They wanted to kill me. I was badly hurt, but I escaped and ran into the open country.

Later, I found an empty hut, which was built against the wall of a small house. I was afraid to go into the house after what had happened in the village, so I hid in the hut. There I was safe, and could escape from the cold, and hide from people who wished to hurt me.

And then I found that there was a small hole in the wall between the hut and the house. Through this hole I could see into the room next to the hut. Three people lived in the house – a beautiful girl, an old man, and a young man.

Day after day I watched the three people. I saw how kind they were to each other. I wanted so much to go into the house and be with them, but I knew I must stay in the hut. I could not forget how the village people had hurt me when I tried to go into the house there.

The people shouted and threw stones at me.

Each night, after the people in the house had gone to bed, I stole some of their food for myself. But soon I realized that the old man was blind. And I realized too that often the three of them did not have enough to eat. I saw the two young people put extra food on the blind man's plate, although they were hungry themselves.

When I saw that, I stopped stealing their food. Their life was already hard enough, so I went back to the wild fruit in the woods. I tried to help them in other ways, too. During the night I cut firewood for them, and added it secretly to the wood which the young man had cut during the day. I was very happy to see how much this pleased the young man.

After a while I began to understand some of the noises that the people made to each other. The first words that I understood were words like 'fire', and 'bread'. I also learnt that the three people called each other by names. The girl was Agatha, the young man was Felix, and the old man was called Father. I tried to make the noises that they made, and slowly I began to speak.

The two young people were very beautiful. One day I saw my own face in the water of the river. It was a terrible face. I understood why people were frightened, why they shouted and threw stones. I knew then that I could not let these beautiful people see me. They would be frightened by my horrible face and body.

Summer was coming, and I continued to watch and learn. I also continued to help the two people and their father,

One day I saw my own face in the water of the river.
It was a terrible face.

and did many jobs for them in the night. They were always surprised in the morning when they saw what I had done. I heard them talk about the 'good creature' who did these 'wonderful' things.

But the family were often sad, and I wished I could make them happy. I looked forward to the time when I could speak well enough to talk to them. And I was happy because I was sure I would soon have three good friends.

8

One day in summer a lady on horseback rode up to the house and knocked on the door. She had dark hair, and was very beautiful. The family were all very pleased to see her. I soon learnt that her name was Sophie.

She could not speak the family's language, and each evening Felix taught her some words. This was a very great help to me, because I was able to learn the meaning of many words that I had not been able to understand before. Felix taught Sophie from books about what had happened in the world in the past. So I learnt about the Greeks and Romans, and about Christ, and about the first white men in America and the sad story of the Indians. I could not understand why men who knew all about good and evil could hate and kill each other.

I learnt other things too. I learnt that people think it is very important to have money and to come from a good family. I learnt of the love between mother and father and child. And I realized that I had no family. The more I learnt, the more I thought, and the more unhappy I became.

Soon I discovered who Sophie was. The two families had met in France after Sophie and her father arrived there from Turkey, their own country. Sophie's father was put in prison by the French, but Felix and his father had helped him to escape and leave France. When the French discovered this, Felix and his family lost all their lands and money, and had to leave France for ever. Now I knew why they were so sad, and why they were poor.

But that was not all. Sophie and Felix loved each other, and Sophie's father had promised that they could marry. Then, when he learnt that Felix had lost all his money, he broke his promise. But Sophie loved Felix very much, so she took some money and escaped from her father to search for Felix.

I had learnt to love these good people and I could not wait another day to introduce myself. I decided to speak first to the father, because he was blind, and would not be frightened by my terrible face and body.

One day the three young people went for a walk while the old man rested. When they had gone, I went to the door of the house and knocked on it.

The old man told me to enter, and to sit down.

'Thank you,' I said. 'I am a traveller, and I'm tired and sad. I have no family or friends. The people that I want to have as my friends have never seen me. If they don't take me into their home, I shall be alone in the world.'

'Don't be so sad,' the old man said. 'You will find that the hearts of men are full of love. If these friends are good people, they will welcome you.'

'They are kind, and the best people in the world,' I said. 'But when they meet me, they may not see a kind creature who has helped them. Instead they may see a monster, and they will hate me.'

'That mustn't happen,' the old man said. 'My family and I have had our difficult times, and we'll help you.'

'You are a very good man,' I said, 'and if you help me, I shall be able to live with my friends and enjoy their love.'

At that moment I heard the young people returning from their walk. I caught the old man's hand, and cried, 'Now is the time! Save me and help me! You and your family are the friends that I am talking about.'

Then the door opened, and in came Felix, Sophie, and Agatha. Their faces were filled with horror and fear when they saw me. Agatha fainted, and Sophie ran out of the house. Felix ran forward and pulled me away from his father. He threw me to the ground and hit me again and again with his heavy stick. I did not lift a hand against him. I did not want to hurt him – or any of them. My heart was heavy, and all hope left me. I ran out of the house and later returned silently to my hut. Nobody saw me.

*Felix threw me to the ground and hit me again and again
with his heavy stick.*

9

I sat in my dark hut, and felt both angry and sad. One half of me wanted to hurt the people who had hurt me. The other half of me still loved them. In the end I decided to try to speak to the old man again. I fell into an unhappy sleep, but when I woke in the morning, the family had gone. They had left the house during the night.

I knew the name of only one other person. Although I had seen you, Frankenstein, for only a few moments, I knew that I belonged to you. When I had left your house, I had picked up a small bag. There was a book in the bag, and I could now read it. From it I learnt my creator's name and address. You had made me, but why had you not looked after me, and saved me from this pain and unhappiness? I decided to go to Geneva, to find you.

One day as I was travelling, I saw a young girl running along the side of a river. Suddenly she fell into the water. I jumped into the river, fought against the fast-moving water, and brought her back to land. While I was doing this, the girl's father, who was looking for her, reached us. He was carrying a gun, and when he saw me, he fired. The bullet hit my arm and broke it. I fell to the ground in great pain, and the man and the girl ran into the woods as fast as they could, and left me.

The bullet was deep in my arm, and I lost a lot of blood. After some days my arm began to get better, but I became sadder and angrier than before. I had saved the girl's life, and how did they thank me? With a bullet in the arm! I began to realize that there was no happiness for me in life. Hate grew stronger in me every day. Hate for you, my creator, who had made me.

Two months later, I reached Geneva. That evening I hid among some trees outside the town, and went to sleep. But I woke when a little boy ran into my hiding place. I thought I would catch the child and make him my friend before he was old enough to be frightened of my terrible face. I caught the little boy, but when the child saw me, he covered his eyes with his hands and screamed loudly.

'Let me go, you monster,' the child shouted. 'Let me go, or I will tell my father, Mr Frankenstein. He will call the police, and they'll punish you.'

'Frankenstein!' I shouted. 'You belong to my enemy, the man that I want to hurt.'

The child fought and screamed, and I put my hand round his neck to stop him shouting. In a moment, the child lay dead at my feet. I looked down at his body, and was pleased with what I had done. I knew that the death of this child would hurt you, Victor Frankenstein, my creator.

Then I saw something bright round the child's neck. It was a gold chain, and on the end of it was a picture of a very beautiful woman. I knew that a beautiful woman would never smile at me, and I wanted to run into Geneva and kill as many people as I could. But I stopped myself,

I put my hand round the child's neck to stop him shouting.
In a moment, he lay dead at my feet.

and went to look for another hiding place. Soon I found a hut, which seemed to be empty, but when I entered I saw a pretty young woman asleep on the floor. I hated her because she was pretty. So I put the gold chain into one of her pockets, and then, before she could wake up, I ran away. I knew the police would think that she had killed the little boy.

Victor Frankenstein continues his Story

10

The monster finished telling me his story, and then he said:

'I am alone and miserable. Only someone as ugly as I am could love me. You must make another creature like me, a woman monster to be my wife.'

'I shall never make another creature like you,' I shouted. 'You have done enough evil on your own.'

'If you don't help me, I shall make you more miserable than you have ever been in your life. You will wish you were dead,' the monster said. 'But if you make another monster to be my friend, we won't hurt anyone. Be kind to me now, and I will learn to love and be kind.'

I thought long and hard about the monster's words. I felt

I thought long and hard about the monster's words.

sorry for him. He was so miserable. Perhaps I should help him.

'I shall do what you ask,' I told him. 'But you must promise to live somewhere in the world where nobody lives. You must promise to stay away from other people.'

'I promise! I promise!' he cried. 'Please start your work. I shall watch you, and when you are ready, you can be sure I will come back.' He turned and left me, and ran down the mountain.

I went back to Geneva immediately. My family were very worried when they saw me. I was pale and my eyes were wild. I could not forget my promise to the monster, and the awful work that waited for me. But I had to do it. It was the only way to keep my family safe . . . safe from his murdering hands around their necks.

I needed to study for several months to make a woman monster successfully. I heard that an English scientist had done some useful work, so I decided to go to England.

Before I went, my father asked me: 'Are you going to marry Elizabeth, or do you love another woman? Is this why you are so unhappy?'

'No, father,' I replied. 'I have always loved Elizabeth, and I want to marry her. But I must do one more piece of scientific work before we can marry. I must go to England to do the work and I want to marry Elizabeth when I return.'

My father and Elizabeth did not want me to go to England alone, because I had been so ill. They spoke to my old friend Henry Clerval, and he was very happy to travel with me. I was pleased that he could come, although I did not want him to discover anything about my horrible work.

Henry and I reached London in early October and stayed there for a few months. I met and talked with English scientists, and learnt many useful things from them. Then Henry was invited to visit some friends in Scotland. I planned to travel with him, but I told him that I wanted to go walking in the mountains alone. Henry was not happy with my plan, but in the end he agreed.

I bought all that I needed for a laboratory, and sent everything to Scotland. Henry and I travelled to Edinburgh together, and then I went further north, to find a good place for my laboratory. At last I found the right place on an island off the north coast. It was a wild and lonely place. Only five people lived on the island, so I could

The island was a wild and lonely place.

work alone, and nobody would discover my awful secret.

There was a large, empty hut on the island, and I brought builders from Scotland to make the hut into a laboratory for me. I showed them how to build my mast, and soon everything was ready for me to start work on the woman monster.

11

One evening two months later I was sitting in my laboratory. Most of my work was done, and I could finish the woman monster that night. But I wondered if I should finish the work.

Was I making a monster more evil than the first creature? Perhaps a thousand times more evil. How could I know? Perhaps the woman monster would be another murderer. She had not promised to stay away from other people. Perhaps the two monsters would hate each other . . . and would kill, and murder, and destroy . . . without end.

As I thought these things, I looked up at the window. Suddenly, in the moonlight, I saw the monster's awful face looking at me. And in his yellow eyes I could see only hate and evil. I knew he would not keep his promise.

I went over to the laboratory table where the new creature was lying. I pulled off the wires that joined her to my machine. I took a sharp knife and cut through the body that I had joined together so carefully. Through the window the monster saw me destroy his woman. With a loud and miserable scream of sadness and lost hope, he ran into the laboratory.

'You have destroyed all my hopes of happiness,' he cried. 'You have left me with one feeling – hate . . . and with one wish – to destroy your happiness. You will be sorry that you were ever born. Remember this: I shall be with you on your wedding night.'

He ran quickly out of the laboratory, and I watched him as he left the island in his boat and sailed away across the sea.

I sat and cried as I thought of the danger to Elizabeth. But I knew that the monster would not visit us until our wedding night. I would not die easily, and I would try to kill him before he could kill me.

The next morning I received a letter from Henry. He

I took a sharp knife and cut through the body that I had joined together so carefully.

told me that he was waiting for me to return. I decided to clear the laboratory and to leave the island on the following day. So I returned to the laboratory, where the pieces of the woman monster's body still lay on the floor. I put them all in a large bag with some heavy stones. Then I took the bag to my boat and sailed out to sea. I threw the bag into deep water, and watched it disappear.

I was happier than I had felt for months. I knew I had done the right thing, and now there would be no second monster to follow the first.

I was very tired, and I went to sleep in the boat. I do not know how long I slept, but when I woke up, I was in the middle of a storm. The wind was driving me further out to sea and my boat began to fill with water. I knew I was in great danger. After some hours the storm passed, and I saw land to the south. Soon I could see the beach . . . and a crowd of people standing and watching me. Their faces were cold and unfriendly.

As I landed, four of the men came towards me and took me by the arms.

'We are taking you to Mr Kerwin, the judge. He wants to ask you some questions about the murder of a man here last night,' one of the men told me.

I was sad to hear of the murder, but I did not worry about it. I had been far away at the time, and knew nothing about any murder. It would be easy to explain that. So I went with the men to the large house where Judge Kerwin lived.

I threw the bag into deep water, and watched it disappear.

12

The judge was an old, kind man, but his face was very serious as he looked at me. He asked a number of men to tell me what they had seen and found the night before.

The first man told his story. He and his son were coming home from a long day's fishing. It was a dark night, and on the beach they had fallen over the dead body of a man. They had carried the body to the nearest house, and found that it was a good-looking young man about twenty-five years old. There were the marks of fingers round his neck. When they spoke of the marks of fingers, I remembered the murder of my brother and I felt a terrible fear.

The son then told his story. He had seen a boat with a man in it, not far from the beach. He thought it was my boat. A woman had also seen a man in a boat sailing away from the beach. She thought I was the man.

Then I was taken to the room where the dead body lay. How can I tell you what I felt when I saw the body? I put my arms round it and cried: 'What have I done? My friend! My dear friend!' The body was Henry Clerval's, and so now I had destroyed another person.

This third death was too much for me. I fell down in a kind of madness, and they had to carry me from the room. For two months I was very ill and wished only to die. But

The fishermen carried the body to the nearest house.

slowly my madness left me, and my health began to return. At last I was able to speak to Judge Kerwin, and I asked for news of my family.

'There is someone here who can answer your question better than I can,' he said. 'Your father arrived a few minutes ago, and is waiting to see you.'

For the first time since Henry's death I felt some happiness. I held out my hands to my father as he came into the room, and he took me in his arms. He gave me the good news that Elizabeth and Ernest were safe and well.

I was really too ill to travel, but I asked my father to take me home immediately. The police had found somebody who had seen me on my island at the time of the murder, and so the judge let me go free.

My father looked after me on the long journey home, and sat with me for every minute. Night after night while I was asleep, I shouted that I was the murderer of William, Justine, and Henry. My father asked me why I said these awful things. I wanted to answer his question, but I could not tell him my terrible secret. He thought that I was still a little mad.

We stayed for a few days in Paris on the way home, and Elizabeth wrote to me at our hotel. This is what her letter said:

My dearest Victor,
I am so happy to know that you will soon be home.

43

But I am afraid that Henry's death is not the only reason for your sadness. Do you still want to marry me, or do you love another woman? You must tell me.

I love you, Victor, and I dream of the day when I shall be your wife. But I do not want you to marry me just because your parents wanted it. I can only be happy if you are happy.

Do not answer this letter. Wait until you arrive before you give me your answer. But if you are well, and if I can make you smile, I need nothing more to make me happy.

> With all my love,
> Elizabeth

I replied immediately. I told her that I loved her very much and wanted to marry her.

I remembered the monster's promise to be with me on the night of my wedding. Let him come. We would fight to the death on that night. And after that fight, I would either be dead and at peace, or alive and free . . . free to be happy with Elizabeth.

We arrived in Geneva soon after my letter had reached Elizabeth. It was wonderful to see her again. She ran into my arms and I held her close. She cried when she saw how thin and old I looked. She, too, was thinner because she had worried about me so much. But her gentleness and her love made her as beautiful as ever.

'I love you, Victor, and I dream of the day when I shall
be your wife.'

We agreed that the wedding would be in ten days' time. As the day came nearer, I became more and more afraid. I tried to hide my fear, and laughed and smiled as often as I could. Elizabeth knew that I was unhappy, but she was sure she could give me happiness. She looked forward to our wedding.

I began to carry a gun and a knife with me everywhere I went.

13

After the wedding a large number of our friends came to a party at our house. When the party had started, Elizabeth and I said goodbye and left for our honeymoon. We travelled first by boat, and planned to spend the night at a hotel on the other side of the lake. The mountains and

The mountains and the lake were calm and beautiful, and at last Elizabeth and I were together.

the lake were calm and beautiful, and at last Elizabeth and I were together. For the first time for months, and for the last time ever, I enjoyed the feeling of happiness.

In the evening the wind became stronger and soon a great storm broke above us. Every noise frightened me, and I kept my hand on my gun under my coat. I saw the monster in every shadow. Suddenly I realized how terrible the fight would be for Elizabeth. I asked her to go to bed and I decided to search for the monster. I planned to join her when I was sure he was not in or around the hotel.

Elizabeth left me and I searched every corner of the hotel – every dark doorway and staircase. I could not find him, and I began to hope that he had not followed us to the hotel. But suddenly, I heard a loud and terrible scream.

It came from our room.

Then – too late – I understood. The monster had promised to be with me on my wedding night, but he had not planned to kill *me*.

The scream came again, and I ran to our room. Why did I not die there and then?

On the bed, Elizabeth lay still, in the cold sleep of death. I took her in my arms . . . and saw the marks of the murderer's fingers on her neck.

Other people in the hotel had heard the screams and came into our room. I sent one of them to call the police. The others left me alone with my misery. I held Elizabeth

On the bed, Elizabeth lay still, in the cold sleep of death.

close, and as I held her, I saw the monster watching me through the open window of the room. There was an evil laugh on his face. I pulled my gun from my coat and fired at him. I missed, and he ran from the window and jumped into the lake. The other people heard the noise of the shot and came back into the room. I showed them the place where the monster had jumped into the lake. We searched the edge of the lake, but we could not find him. I returned to our room and lay on the bed next to my dear wife.

Suddenly I had another terrible thought. At this very moment perhaps my father was fighting the monster, with Ernest dead at his feet.

I left the hotel and returned to Geneva as fast as I could. My father and Ernest were safe, but the awful news of Elizabeth's death killed my father. He had loved Elizabeth dearly. He became ill, and after a few days he died in my arms. So the evil monster had brought unhappiness and death to a dear old man who had never hurt anybody.

I do not know what happened next. I think I left the real world, and entered a dangerous world of dreams and madness. Later I found that they had put me in prison because of my madness.

After many months they let me free. I had only one wish – to find and kill the monster.

14

I decided to leave Geneva for ever. I took all the money that I needed, and left the town. Before I left, I went to visit the place where William, Elizabeth, and my father lay at rest. I stood there and promised them that I would stay alive until I had killed the monster.

A loud, evil laugh rang out through the silent night. Then I heard the monster's voice: 'It pleases me that you have decided to live, because that is just what I want.'

I ran towards the voice, but I could not catch the monster. I saw him running away, but he ran faster than any man could go – too fast for me to catch. But I followed him, and I have been following him since that day. I shall stay alive until I can catch him. He wants me to live as long as possible. He wants me to feel, day after day, the pain and misery that he has given me. He leaves messages to tell me where he is. He knows that I shall follow him.

I am only happy when I am asleep. I dream that I am with my family, and Elizabeth and Henry. When I am awake, I look forward to my death, to the day when I shall be with them.

In his last message the monster told me that he was going north. He wanted to take me where the cold would hurt me and make me more miserable. I followed him to the cold lands of the north, and bought dogs and a sledge.

I followed the monster to the cold lands of the north.

Until now, he has always left me further and further behind when I chased him. But the dogs were very fast and I was getting closer and closer to him. Soon he was only one day's journey in front of me. He was going towards the sea, and I hoped to catch him before he reached it. The chase over the ice continued for about three weeks. The pain from the cold was very great, and I began to lose hope. I thought I would never catch him. My dogs could not run much further, and one of them died. Then I saw something on the ice in front of me. It was the monster and his sledge. Suddenly I was full of hope again, and I gave a great shout of happiness.

I got closer and closer to him. Then a great storm started. The ice began to break, and the sea carried him away from me. My sledge was broken, and I lost my dogs. I was left on a piece of ice that was becoming smaller all the time. Many hours went by, and then I saw your ship. The rest you know.

I ask you, Captain Walton, to chase the monster and kill him. Do not listen to what he says. He knows how to argue, and perhaps you will feel sorry for him. But remember that he is evil. Remember the deaths of William, Justine, Henry Clerval, Elizabeth, my father . . . and remember me, Victor Frankenstein.

There is no more for me to say, except to thank you, Captain Walton, for your help and kindness. Thank you also for listening to my story. I want you to tell the world that the monster is a danger to everyone.

I know that I have only a few hours left to live, but I can feel my loved ones near me, and I welcome death.

Goodbye. This is the end of Victor Frankenstein's story.

Many hours went by, and then I saw your ship.

Captain Walton's Note

15

I, Captain Robert Walton, have added this final note to the story. When you have read it, you will know that Victor Frankenstein's story was true.

Victor Frankenstein died a few hours after he had written his last word. I was sad to see him die, because he had become a good friend. But he will not be unhappy or in pain any more, and I am happy for him.

We laid his body in a cabin near my own. Later I heard a voice coming from the cabin. I went into the cabin and saw a huge shape standing over the dead body. I knew that the horrible creature which was standing there was Frankenstein's monster.

'So I have killed you, too,' the monster said to Frankenstein's body. 'Oh, Frankenstein, forgive me. How I wish you could answer me.'

I went towards him, and said: 'It is too late for Frankenstein to forgive you. He is dead. His pain is ended.'

'You do not know how much pain and unhappiness I have felt,' said the monster. 'I knew that I was doing evil things, but I could not stop myself. Do you think I enjoyed killing people? My heart was made for love, like a man's heart. After I killed Henry Clerval, I hated myself. But I could not stop myself from more murder. Frankenstein would not give me a wife, but he hoped to find happiness with a wife of his own. He was not fair to me. But now it is ended. Frankenstein is the last person I shall kill.

'I have done all those evil things, but am I the only person who has done wrong? I wanted love and friendship. Think about Felix and his family, who hated me after I had given them love. Think about the man who shot me after I had saved his little girl from the river. But I know that I have done evil, and I hate myself more than you hate me. My own death is near. I shall leave this ship and go north, across the ice. I shall build a great fire, and lie down on it to die. I shall welcome the pain of the fire, because it will help me to forget the pain in my heart. I have felt more pain than Frankenstein. And when the fire has died down, I shall be at peace.'

'I shall go north, across the ice,' said the monster.

The monster jumped from the cabin window as he said this. He got into the small boat in which he had reached the ship. The sea soon carried him away, and he was lost in the darkness.

GLOSSARY

believe to think that something or someone is true or right

blind *(adj)* not able to see

cabin a room on a ship

chain *(n)* a row of very small gold rings joined together, to wear round the neck

create to make something new

creature a living animal or person

electricity the power that travels through wires and can make heat and light and drive machines

evil *(adj)* very bad

faint *(v)* to fall down suddenly because you are ill or hurt

float *(v)* to stay on the top of water

forgive to say or show that you are not angry with someone any more

great very big; special, very important

honeymoon a holiday for a new husband and wife after their wedding

horrible terrible; making you very afraid

horror a feeling of very strong fear and dislike

huge very, very big

hut a small building made of stone or wood, usually with one room

human *(adj)* of people, not animals

judge *(n)* the most important person at a trial, who decides how to punish a criminal

laboratory a building where scientists work and study

lightning a sudden, very bright light in the sky during a storm

look after to take care of someone or something

mad   ill in the head

mark *(n)*   when you touch something, your fingers can leave a
mark, which shows where you have touched

mast   a very tall wooden or metal post

monster   an animal or person in stories which is big, ugly, and
frightening

ordinary   usual, not special

point *(v)*   to show with your finger or hand where something is

power   something strong that makes other things work, e.g.
electric power

professor   an important teacher at a university

scientific   of science

scientist   someone who studies science, which is the study of
natural things, e.g. biology, chemistry, physics

sledge   a kind of 'car' without wheels, that moves on long
pieces of wood or metal over snow

strangle   to kill someone by holding them very hard round the
neck

telescope   an instrument with special glass for looking at things
which are a long way away

throw (past tense **threw**)   to move your arm quickly to send
something through the air

thunder   a very loud noise in the sky during a storm

trial   a meeting (in a law court) to decide if someone has done a
crime

ugly   not beautiful; not nice to look at

wire *(n)*   a long thin piece of metal; electricity travels through
wires

Frankenstein

ACTIVITIES

Before Reading

1 Read the story introduction on the first page of the book, and the back cover. What do you know now about this story? Choose the best words to complete this passage.

Victor Frankenstein is a *monster / scientist*. He takes parts from *dead / living* people and builds a new *machine / man* with them. This *huge / small* and *beautiful / ugly* monster needs *food / love*, but *everybody / nobody* cares about him, and so he soon learns to *hate / hope*. Because he is *happy / unhappy*, he turns *to / against* the man who created him, and *destroys / steals* everything that Frankenstein loves.

2 Can you guess who will say or think these things in the story – Victor Frankenstein or the monster?

1 'You are an evil creature. I shall kill you if I can.'
2 'You should love me and be kind to me, like a father.'
3 'I am tired and sad. I have no family or friends.'
4 'You will be sorry that you were ever born.'
5 'He wants me to feel, day after day, the pain and misery that he has given me.'
6 'I know that I have only a few hours left to live, but I can feel my loved ones near me, and I welcome death.'
7 'Am I the only person who has done wrong?'
8 'My own death is near . . . I shall welcome the pain of the fire, because it will help me to forget the pain in my heart.'

While Reading

Read Chapter 1. Can you guess the answers to these questions?

1 Is the driver of the first sledge the monster?
2 Why was the second sledge chasing the first one?
3 Where is the 'huge figure' now? Has he escaped?
4 Will the Captain believe Victor Frankenstein's story?

Read Chapters 2 to 4. Are these sentences true (T) or false (F)? Rewrite the false sentences with the correct information.

1 Mrs Frankenstein was Elizabeth's real mother.
2 Victor studied hard, and was interested in electricity.
3 Victor's mother hoped that he would marry Justine.
4 Victor and his friend Henry went to university together.
5 Victor planned to use electricity to help people.
6 He wanted everybody to know the secret of his machine.
7 He was very pleased with the creature that he had made.

Before you read Chapter 5, can you guess what has just happened at Victor's home? Choose Y (Yes), N (No) or P (Perhaps) for each of these ideas.

1 One of his family has had an accident. Y/N/P
2 One of his brothers has run away. Y/N/P
3 The monster has killed one of his family. Y/N/P

Read Chapters 5 and 6, and then match these halves of sentences.

1 William was murdered . . .
2 At the time, William was wearing a gold chain, . . .
3 When Victor saw the monster at the scene of the crime, . . .
4 Victor tried to catch the murderer, . . .
5 The police thought Justine had killed William, . . .
6 Because everyone hated him, . . .
7 Victor realized he had given the monster life, . . .
8 he knew at once who had killed William.
9 but he had not given him love.
10 while he and Ernest were playing in the countryside.
11 so they arrested her and put her on trial.
12 the monster was the unhappiest creature in the world.
13 but the monster could run much faster than any man.
14 which Elizabeth had lent him.

Read Chapters 7 to 9 (*The Monster's Story*). Choose the best question-word for these questions, and then answer them.

Who / What / How

1 . . . did most people do when they saw the monster?
2 . . . did the monster help Felix's family?
3 . . . did the monster learn to speak and read?
4 . . . did the monster want Felix's father to do?
5 . . . shot the monster?
6 . . . strangled William?
7 . . . did the monster do with the gold chain?

Before you read Chapter 10, can you guess which of these two things will happen?

1 Victor will try to love the monster, and teach him to be kind and good.
2 Victor thinks the monster is evil, so he will try to kill him.

Read Chapters 10 to 12. Who said or wrote this, and to whom? What, or who, were they talking about?

1 'You have done enough evil on your own.'
2 'I will learn to love and be kind.'
3 'Is this why you are so unhappy?'
4 'You have destroyed all my hopes of happiness.'
5 'What have I done?'
6 'I can only be happy if you are happy.'

Before you read Chapter 13, can you guess the answers to these questions?

1 Will the monster come to Victor's wedding?
2 Will Elizabeth and Victor get married and be happy?
3 Will the monster try to kill Victor, or Elizabeth?

Read Chapters 13 to 15, and answer these questions.

1 Why did Victor leave the hotel and hurry back to Geneva?
2 Why did he want to stay alive after Elizabeth's death?
3 Why did the monster want Victor to live for a long time?
4 What did Victor ask Captain Walton to do after his death?
5 How did the monster plan to die?

ACTIVITIES

After Reading

1 **What did Felix and his father say after the monster had run away? Complete Felix's part of the conversation. (Use as many words as you like.)**

FATHER: My boy, you were wrong to hit that poor man.

FELIX: But _____.

FATHER: Kill us? Why do you think that?

FELIX: You didn't _____.

FATHER: The poor man can't change his face, Felix. And he didn't *sound* evil to me.

FELIX: What _____?

FATHER: He talked about kindness and love. And he asked for my help because he wanted us to be his friends.

FELIX: Friends? He _____.

FATHER: Perhaps he *looked* like a monster, Felix, but that doesn't mean he had an evil heart.

FELIX: I'm sure _____.

FATHER: But you hit him first – and he didn't fight back.

FELIX: That's because _____.

FATHER: But was it fair to hit him with your stick?

FELIX: Well, I think _____.

FATHER: What! Leave our home! Why should we do that?

FELIX: Because I'm afraid the monster _____.

FATHER: Well, I thought he was just an unhappy, lonely man, not a murderer. But if you say we must go, then we'll go.

2 **When the monster followed Victor to Britain, what was he thinking? Fill in the gaps with these words.**

alive, broken, create, destroyed, electricity, followed, forgive, happiness, huge, human, hurt, island, keep, laboratory, lightning, lonely, machine, mast, monster, moonlight, sharp, sorry, wires

I was so happy when Frankenstein agreed to _____ a woman _____ for me! With a wife, I would never be _____ again, or want to _____ anybody. I wanted to be sure that Frankenstein would _____ his promise, so I _____ him to England, and then to a Scottish _____. He built his _____ and a tall _____ above it, which would bring the _____ from _____ down to his machine. Then he built a _____ woman from parts of _____ bodies, and I waited happily to see her come _____.

But one night he saw my face in the _____ outside the window. Suddenly he pulled off the _____ that joined her to the _____, took a _____ knife and cut through her body. In one moment, he _____ my wife, and all my hopes of _____.

I cannot _____ him for this. He has _____ his promise to me, and I shall make him _____ that he was ever born. I know just how to do it . . .

3 **Look at these words used in the story. Can you find words that have opposite meanings?**

create   _____   miserable   _____
evil   _____   sadness   _____
horrible   _____   ugly   _____

4 Perhaps Victor's father wrote to Elizabeth on the way home from Scotland. Choose the right endings for the sentences, and join them with these linking words to make the letter.

although / and / because / before / but / so / that / which / why

My dear Elizabeth,

1 You will be happy to hear that Victor and I are now on our way back to Geneva, _____

2 When he gets home, he will need your loving care _____

3 His illness was like a kind of madness, _____

4 I couldn't understand why he said these things, _____

5 He won't tell me what it is, _____

6 There is one last thing I want to say, Elizabeth, _____

7 _____ I have always wanted you two to marry,

8 Perhaps he loves another woman and this is _____

9 But whatever happens, Elizabeth, remember _____

10 perhaps he will tell *you*.

11 made him cry out in his sleep that *he* was the murderer of poor William, Justine and Henry.

12 you will be able to see him very soon.

13 you will always be my dear daughter.

14 I think he is keeping a secret from me.

15 he has been very ill.

16 he is so unhappy.

17 I want you to be sure that Victor really loves you.

18 we arrive home.

Your loving 'father'

5 **Do you agree (A) or disagree (D) with these sentences? Explain why.**

1 Scientists should try new things all the time. If they don't, we will never find new and better ways of living.

2 There are some ideas that scientists should not think about or study; for example, putting an end to a seriously ill person's life, or putting parts of animals into humans.

3 Nobody (doctors, scientists, artists, etc.) should re-use parts of people's dead bodies for any reason.

4 Scientists just want to discover and understand new things. It is not their fault if other people use their scientific discoveries in dangerous or evil ways.

6 **The title of this story is *Frankenstein*. Look at these questions about titles, and discuss your answers.**

1 Does the title make it clear that Frankenstein is the scientist, not the monster? And if it doesn't, is there a reason for this, do you think?

2 How much should a title explain about a story? Should it give information, or be mysterious?

7 **Here are some different titles for the story. Which of them do you prefer to the real title, if any? Can you say why?**

The Monster that Nobody Loved   The Secret of Life

Frankenstein's Monster   An Evil Thing

Death in the Mountains   A Human Monster

The Monster of our Dreams   A Horrible Science

ABOUT THE AUTHOR

Mary Shelley (1797–1851) was the daughter of William Godwin and Mary Wollstonecraft, both writers and famous people of that time. When Mary was sixteen, she ran away to Europe with the famous English poet, Percy Bysshe Shelley, and married him two years later, after his wife's death. For four years they lived in Italy, until Shelley's death in 1822, when Mary returned to England with their son Percy.

She wrote many books during her life, but today she is remembered only for her first novel, *Frankenstein*. The idea for this famous story came to her when she and her husband were staying with Lord Byron, another well-known English poet, at his villa near Lake Geneva. One stormy night Byron suggested that everyone should write a ghost story. At first Mary did not have any ideas, but later she had a dream in which a monster appeared, and so *Frankenstein* was born. When she wrote the novel, she was only nineteen and was expecting a baby. Two of her children had already died young, and we can see in this novel her fears and worries about pregnancy, childbirth, and the way children develop in later life.

Frankenstein is often called the first science-fiction story, and many films have been made of it. Most of them show a 'mad' scientist and an 'evil' monster, as often happens in horror films (for example, the dinosaurs in the film *Jurassic Park*). A recent film (Kenneth Branagh, 1994) is closer to Mary Shelley's story: it shows how a scientist has to make difficult choices, and that the monster is just sad and lonely, not evil at all.

OXFORD BOOKWORMS LIBRARY

Classics • Crime & Mystery • Factfiles • Fantasy & Horror
Human Interest • Playscripts • Thriller & Adventure
True Stories • World Stories

The OXFORD BOOKWORMS LIBRARY provides enjoyable reading in English, with a wide range of classic and modern fiction, non-fiction, and plays. It includes original and adapted texts in seven carefully graded language stages, which take learners from beginner to advanced level. An overview is given on the next pages.

All Stage 1 titles are available as audio recordings, as well as over eighty other titles from Starter to Stage 6. All Starters and many titles at Stages 1 to 4 are specially recommended for younger learners. Every Bookworm is illustrated, and Starters and Factfiles have full-colour illustrations.

The OXFORD BOOKWORMS LIBRARY also offers extensive support. Each book contains an introduction to the story, notes about the author, a glossary, and activities. Additional resources include tests and worksheets, and answers for these and for the activities in the books. There is advice on running a class library, using audio recordings, and the many ways of using Oxford Bookworms in reading programmes. Resource materials are available on the website <www.oup.com/elt/gradedreaders>.

The *Oxford Bookworms Collection* is a series for advanced learners. It consists of volumes of short stories by well-known authors, both classic and modern. Texts are not abridged or adapted in any way, but carefully selected to be accessible to the advanced student.

You can find details and a full list of titles in the *Oxford Bookworms Library Catalogue* and *Oxford English Language Teaching Catalogues*, and on the website <www.oup.com/elt/gradedreaders>.

THE OXFORD BOOKWORMS LIBRARY
GRADING AND SAMPLE EXTRACTS

STARTER • 250 HEADWORDS

present simple – present continuous – imperative –
can/cannot, must – *going to* (future) – simple gerunds …

Her phone is ringing – but where is it?

Sally gets out of bed and looks in her bag. No phone. She looks under the bed. No phone. Then she looks behind the door. There is her phone. Sally picks up her phone and answers it. *Sally's Phone*

STAGE 1 • 400 HEADWORDS

… past simple – coordination with *and, but, or* –
subordination with *before, after, when, because, so* …

I knew him in Persia. He was a famous builder and I worked with him there. For a time I was his friend, but not for long. When he came to Paris, I came after him – I wanted to watch him. He was a very clever, very dangerous man. *The Phantom of the Opera*

STAGE 2 • 700 HEADWORDS

… present perfect – *will* (future) – *(don't) have to, must not, could* –
comparison of adjectives – simple *if* clauses – past continuous –
tag questions – *ask/tell* + infinitive …

While I was writing these words in my diary, I decided what to do. I must try to escape. I shall try to get down the wall outside. The window is high above the ground, but I have to try. I shall take some of the gold with me – if I escape, perhaps it will be helpful later. *Dracula*

STAGE 3 • 1000 HEADWORDS

… should, may – present perfect continuous – *used to* – past perfect –
causative – relative clauses – indirect statements …

Of course, it was most important that no one should see
Colin, Mary, or Dickon entering the secret garden. So Colin
gave orders to the gardeners that they must all keep away
from that part of the garden in future. *The Secret Garden*

STAGE 4 • 1400 HEADWORDS

… past perfect continuous – passive (simple forms) –
would conditional clauses – indirect questions –
relatives with *where/when* – gerunds after prepositions/phrases …

I was glad. Now Hyde could not show his face to the world
again. If he did, every honest man in London would be
proud to report him to the police. *Dr Jekyll and Mr Hyde*

STAGE 5 • 1800 HEADWORDS

… future continuous – future perfect –
passive (modals, continuous forms) –
would have conditional clauses – modals + perfect infinitive …

If he had spoken Estella's name, I would have hit him. I was
so angry with him, and so depressed about my future, that I
could not eat the breakfast. Instead I went straight to the old
house. *Great Expectations*

STAGE 6 • 2500 HEADWORDS

… passive (infinitives, gerunds) – advanced modal meanings –
clauses of concession, condition

When I stepped up to the piano, I was confident. It was as if I
knew that the prodigy side of me really did exist. And when
I started to play, I was so caught up in how lovely I looked
that I didn't worry how I would sound. *The Joy Luck Club*

Tales of Mystery and Imagination

EDGAR ALLAN POE

Retold by Margaret Naudi

The human mind is a dark, bottomless pit, and sometimes it works in strange and frightening ways. That sound in the night . . . is it a door banging in the wind, or a murdered man knocking inside his coffin? The face in the mirror . . . is it yours, or the face of someone standing behind you, who is never there when you turn around?

These famous short stories by Edgar Allan Poe, that master of horror, explore the dark world of the imagination, where the dead live and speak, where fear lies in every shadow of the mind . . .

Tooth and Claw – Short Stories

SAKI

Retold by Rosemary Border

Conradin is ten years old. He lives alone with his aunt. He has two big secrets. The first is that he hates his aunt. The second is that he keeps a small, wild animal in the garden shed. The animal has sharp, white teeth, and it loves fresh blood. Every night, Conradin prays to this animal and asks it to do one thing for him, just one thing.

This collection of short stories is clever, funny, and shows us 'Nature, red in tooth and claw'. In other words, it is Saki at his very best.